CENTER COURT

The History of Basketball

JAIME WINTERS

CRABTREE
Publishing Company
www.crabtreebooks.com

Author: Jaime Winters

Editors: Marcia Abramson, Kelly Spence

Proofreader: Wendy Scavuzzo

Photo research: Melissa McClellan

Design: T.J. Choleva

Cover Design: Samara Parent

Prepress Technician: Tammy McGarr

Production coordinator: Margaret Amy Salter

Written and produced for
Crabtree Publishing by BlueApple*Works* Inc.

Consultant: Greg Verner, President, Ontario Basketball

Cover images: (top) 1960 World Champion Boston Celtics, (bottom left) Kareem Abdul-Jabbar, legendary center for Milwaukee Bucks and Los Angeles Lakers, (bottom center) Sheryl Swoopes, left, Rebecca Lobo, and Lisa Leslie, right, 1996 Olympic Gold Medalists for the United States, (bottom right) James Naismith, inventor of the game of basketball

Photographs

Cover: AP Images: Bill Kostroun (bottom center); Icon Sportswire: Zuma Press (bottom left); Wikimedia Commons: D. Gordon E. Robertson (bottom right), public domaine (top backgroud)

Interior: Shutterstock.com: © Eric Broder Van Dyke (title page, p 12–13 top) © Africa Studio (basketball behind page numbers; © Torsak Thammachote (TOC); © Danny Smythe TOC bottom; © Dewitt (texture background); © Brocreative (page top left); © Eugene Sergeev (page top border); © prophoto14 (page bottom border); © Slavoljub Pantelic (Slam Dunk photo); © Photo smile (p 7 middle bottom); © efecreata mediagroup (p 12–13 bottom); © Aspen Photo (p 15, 20–21 top, 28 right); © Ferenc Szelepcsenyi (p 17 bottom); © efecreata mediagroup p 28–29 top; © FCG (p 28–29 bottom); © Works (p 29 top); © Doug James (p 29 left); © efecreata mediagroup (p 30 bottom); © racorn (p 30 right); © Carlyn Iverson: p 5, p 7 top right, p 7 bottom right, p 10; Keystone Press: © Richard Ulreich (p 23 right); © George Bridges (p 24); Public Domain: TOC top, p 6 top right; p 12 left; p 12 right; p 13 top and bottom; p 19 left; p 20 bottom left; p 21 left; p 21 middle; p 21 right; p 22; p 23 left; p 26 right bottom; p 27 top; p 27 bottom; Library of Congress: title page middle left; New York World-Telegram & Sun Collection (title page middle right); Detroit Publishing Co. (p 4); p 6–7 top; Hersey Photo Service (p 6 bottom, 7 top right, 11 top); Bain Collection (p 6 bottom right, 18); National Photo Company Collection (p 8 left, 8 right); p 11 bottom; p 14 left; Harris & Ewing Collection (p 14 right); Farm Security Administration/Office of War Information Black-and-White Negatives (p 16); New York World-Telegram and the Sun Newspaper Photograph Collection (p 20 top left); p 26 left; National Library of Scotland: p 9 top; National Library of France: p 9 bottom; The Sports Agent/MyStockPhoto.com (p 17 top); Stanford University Archives: p 26; The U.S. Army: p 19 right; Creative Commons: El Pantera (p 20–21 bottom); Rico Shen (p 25)

Library and Archives Canada Cataloguing in Publication

Winters, Jaime, author
     Center court : the history of basketball / Jaime Winters.

(Basketball source)
Includes index.
Issued in print and electronic formats.
ISBN 978-0-7787-1535-1 (bound).--
ISBN 978-0-7787-1539-9 (paperback).--
ISBN 978-1-4271-7753-7 (pdf).--ISBN 978-1-4271-7749-0 (html)

     1. Basketball--History--Juvenile literature. I. Title.

GV883.W56 2015   j796.323   C2015-903196-6
                                          C2015-903197-4

Library of Congress Cataloging-in-Publication Data

Winters, Jaime.
     Center court : the history of basketball / Jaime Winters.
       pages cm. -- (Basketball Source)
     Includes index.
     ISBN 978-0-7787-1535-1 (reinforced library binding : alk. paper) --
     ISBN 978-0-7787-1539-9 (paperback : alk. paper) --
     ISBN 978-1-4271-7753-7 (electronic PDF) --
     ISBN 978-1-4271-7749-0 (electronic HTML)
     1. Basketball--History--Juvenile literature. I. Title.
     GV885.1.W555 2016
     796.323--dc23
                                          2015021128

Crabtree Publishing Company

www.crabtreebooks.com   1-800-387-7650

Printed in Canada/082015/BF20150630

Published in Canada
Crabtree Publishing
616 Welland Ave.
St. Catharines, ON
L2M 5V6

Published in the United States
Crabtree Publishing
PMB 59051
350 Fifth Avenue, 59th Floor
New York, New York 10118

Published in the United Kingdom
Crabtree Publishing
Maritime House
Basin Road North, Hove
BN41 1WR

Published in Australia
Crabtree Publishing
3 Charles Street
Coburg North
VIC 3058

CONTENTS

TAKE IT TO THE NET!

THE NEW GAME ON THE BLOCK

How was basketball invented? Unlike baseball and soccer, hoops didn't come from an ancient game or sport. A teacher made it up, when he had a bored gym class on his hands!

INVENTOR OF BASKETBALL

In 1891, an **unruly** gym class at the **YMCA** (the Y) in Springfield, Massachusetts, drove two teachers to quit. But that didn't stop James Naismith from taking them on. The young teacher thought the dull exercises the students were doing was the problem—not the kids. So Naismith, a star athlete from McGill University in Montreal, Canada, shook things up with indoor football. But it was too rough. Indoor soccer and Naismith's favorite game lacrosse didn't work either. The kids needed a new sport.

Basketball's birthplace is in southwest Massachusetts, near Hartford, Connecticut. The site was a YMCA training center until 1954, when it became Springfield College.

SLAM DUNK!

When a student suggested naming the game "Naismith Ball," Naismith said that would "kill the game." The student then suggested "Basket Ball" and the name stuck.

4

THE FIRST GAME

Naismith thought back to games he had played as a kid. Inspiration struck and he wrote out 13 rules for a new game. The next day, he posted the rules on the bulletin board and nailed two peach baskets 10 feet (3 meters) above the gym floor. He told the class the object of the game was to shoot a soccer ball into their opponents' basket. He tossed the ball into the air, two teams jumped up for it, and the game began. Nobody knew how to throw the ball into the basket. Eventually, one shot went in. It was the only goal of the game, but the class was hooked!

Naismith asked for square baskets to use for goals, but the school janitor found some round peach baskets instead.

DUCK ON A ROCK

Naismith's idea for basketball came from a game he played as a child called Duck on a Rock. Just like basketball, Duck on a Rock includes guarding a goal, throwing at a target, and shooting from behind a line. To play, kids put a large stone, called a duck, on top of a big rock or a tree stump. One player guards the duck. The others stand behind a line and take turns throwing smaller stones at it. There are different rules for what happens if a player misses the duck or knocks it down, but in all of them, the guard must try to tag another player. That player then becomes the new guard.

In Duck on a Rock, a soft lob shot was more likely to knock down the duck than a straight hard throw. Remembering this helped Naismith invent his new game of basketball.

Naismith hung the peach baskets from a **roman balcony** in the gym. The hard, wooden gym floor became the first basketball court. But as the game spread, the court, the baskets, and even the ball changed greatly.

COURT NOT FIT FOR KINGS

Games began popping up almost anywhere—in the great outdoors, church basements, dance halls, and even bars. The ball often flew into windows, stairs, and walls on these **makeshift** courts. That meant players could run into these **hazards**, too, along with broken glass. Also, teams could have anywhere from 3 to 40 players, depending on how many people wanted to play. Referees often had a tough time seeing fouls to call penalties.

The first basketball court was indoors, so students could play during the cold Massachusetts winter.

Basketball spread quickly because there were few rules for the early game and courts could be set up easily.

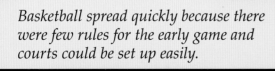

6

ALL HAD A BALL

Many early games were played with soccer balls, but even a football would do since the original rules did not permit players to bounce the ball. When the rules changed to allow bouncing the ball before passing it on, players found soccer balls were too slippery for dribbling and ball handling. In 1894, the first official basketball was made. It was wider than a soccer ball and a bit bigger than a modern basketball. Early balls were made of leather panels stitched together. Today, balls are made of rubber, which gives the ball its bounce.

As the game grew popular, peach baskets were replaced in 1906 by metal hoops and backboards.

When the ball was shot in to a peach basket, it stayed there. At first referees climbed a ladder to get the ball back. Then holes were cut in basket bottoms so they could poke it out with a stick. It wasn't long before a net appeared with a cord that referees could pull to make the ball drop out.

In the 1950s, basketballs were changed from brown to orange so fans could see them better.

SLAM DUNK!

The NBA's official ball made by Spalding has 122 "pebbles" per square inch on the surface. Pebbles are raised dots that help players grip the ball. The dots are stamped onto the ball's surface.

YMCA SPREADS THE GAME

The exciting new game of basketball buzzed throughout the college. Students flocked to the Y every day at lunchtime to watch the action on the court, and basketball took off.

FROM THE Y TO THE WORLD

Over Christmas, when students returned home for the holidays, they introduced the game to friends in other states and Canada. In January 1892, a newspaper published by the Y ran a story explaining the rules, moves, and equipment. Overnight, more than 200 Ys began holding games, and players and fans took it overseas. In 1893, basketball landed in Europe, where a game was held in Paris. Players also brought the game to China, Japan, and Persia (modern-day Iran).

Kids of all ages started playing basketball all over the world.

HOOPS FOR TROOPS

As basketball spread to Ys everywhere, it caught on with gym teachers. Not only was the game fun to play, but it was also an excellent workout. Gym teachers, including Naismith, helped U.S. forces to learn and to play the game wherever they went during World War I (1914–1918). As people watched the soldiers play, basketball picked up more fans and spread through Europe. During the war, James Naismith went to a Y in Paris, where he noticed that the games played by American soldiers sparked lots of interest in the sport.

Soldiers from other countries such as the United Kingdom learned basketball from U.S. forces during World War I.

After the war, basketball was played at the Inter-Allied Military Games in Paris in 1919.

THE WORLD GETS GAME

In 1932, the first international basketball meeting took place with representatives from ten countries. They standardized the rules and formed the FIBA— Fédération Internationale de Basketball Amateur, or the International Basketball Federation. By 1936, basketball was an Olympic sport.

COMPETITION RULES THE GAME

Fierce competition soon fired up the court. Local teams and leagues sprung up in cities such as New York, Philadelphia, and Boston. Every team wanted to be the best hoopsters on the block.

THE FIRST PRO GAME

Around 1892, some young men in Trenton, New Jersey, formed their own basketball team that crushed all the competition. No team at the Y or any local college could beat the Trenton Basketball Team (TBT). In 1896, they took on the Brooklyn YMCA—the champions of New York—in their season opener. The TBT rented a gym, ran ads, and sold more than 600 tickets at 15 to 25 cents apiece for the game. Each team sent seven players to go head-to-head on the court. Still the game was no contest. TBT demolished Brooklyn 16 to 1. After they paid the rent, the players had money left over to pay themselves.

The 1896-1897 Trentons won the unofficial national title with a record of 19 wins and 1 loss.

A LEAGUE IS BORN

In 1898, the first pro basketball league formed. The National Basket Ball League (NBBL) had six teams in and around Trenton and Philadelphia. But by the end of the season, two teams had **folded** and only four remained. The Trenton Nationals won the first two league championships, and the New York Wanderers won the third. The league folded in its sixth season.

Players in the NBBL earned about only $12 a game. The league had money problems and had to shut down.

PROS COME AND GO

The NBBL wasn't the only pro league that sprung up in the eastern states. But they all had a short life span. Some died after only a few seasons, and none lasted more than seven.

CITY OF BASKETBALL LOVE

By 1898, basketball had become so popular in Philadelphia, Pennsylvania, that three of the original six teams in the new National Basket Ball League were from the City of Brotherly Love, as the city is nicknamed.

Many NBBL games were played in Philadelphia, where the art museum (above) is a famous landmark.

FROM AMATEUR TO PRO

As pro league basketball evolved, so did the game. Basketball players went from being amateur athletes to pros who were paid top dollar to play the game.

PAY FOR PLAY

Unlike pro athletes, amateurs are not paid to play sports. But that wasn't always so with basketball. When Y teams played against each other, players were paid for their expenses and star players were paid extra. All players had regular day jobs to make a living. Basketball's first pros, the Trenton Basketball Team, got paid $5 to $15 a game. As pro leagues formed, teams fought for top players, and players could play for whoever offered top dollar. Some players even played for the top-paying team in more than one league at once!

ED WACHTER

Hall of famer Ed Wachter played center on pro teams from 1899 to 1924, then coached college basketball for another 25 years.

From 1908 to 1910, the Buffalo Germans shot to fame, winning 111 games in a row. But some said they weren't the top pro team around, because they often played against weak teams.

FATHERS OF BASKETBALL

In 1918, businessman James Furey put together the Original Celtics with a lineup of star players. Furey had all the players sign **exclusive** contracts, so they couldn't play for other teams. The pro team became the Fathers of Basketball, inventing plays and moves as they toured the United States. One season, the Celtics played 205 games across the country, winning 193, tying 1, and losing only 11. The team's biggest stars were floor leader Nat Holman, center Joe Lapchick, and John Beckman, a deadly shooter. All three were elected to the Basketball Hall of Fame. When Beckman signed with the Original Celtics, he became one of the team's top scorers. His almost perfect ability to put **free throws** in the basket earned him the nickname the "Babe Ruth of Basketball."

JOE **LAPCHICK**

After anchoring the Original Celtics at center, Lapchick became a much-admired coach for St. John's University and the New York Knicks.

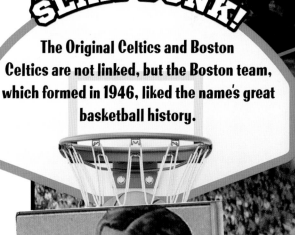

SLAM DUNK!

The Original Celtics and Boston Celtics are not linked, but the Boston team, which formed in 1946, liked the name's great basketball history.

Holman earned the nickname "Mr. Basketball" because he was not only a great player, but was a top coach at the same time. He coached City College of New York during the week and played for the Celtics on weekends.

NAT **HOLMAN**

COLLEGE BASKETBALL

By 1893, basketball had spread from the Y to colleges. Male and female students were eager to get in the game, and it became one of their favorite ways to pass the time between classes.

STUDENTS JUMP UP

In 1896, Yale University formed a basketball squad that took on many of the Y's top East Coast teams. The Yale squad also hit the road to challenge other colleges in the Midwest and beyond. This sparked many colleges to get in the game. That same year, the first women's game between two colleges took place. Defense ruled the court as the women of Stanford University won the low-scoring game against the University of California by a score of 2 to 1.

In basketball's early days, women wore divided skirts called bloomers. Ladies did not wear shorts or pants at that time.

MAD ABOUT THE GAME

In 1905, 15 colleges formed the first basketball rules committee. In 1910, the National Collegiate Athletic Association (NCAA) started governing college sports. The high level of play drew many fans to college games. Sometimes fans had to be turned away. In 1939, the NCAA ran a national tournament that made even more people excited about the college game. Today, the NCAA tournament is known as March Madness and millions of fans watch it on TV.

Only 68 men's teams and 64 women's teams get invited to the "Big Dance," another name for the NCAA championships.

SLAM DUNK!

On February 9, 1895, the first basketball game between two colleges was played on a handball court in the basement of a science building. The Minnesota School of Agriculture beat Hamline College 9 to 3.

AFRICAN-AMERICAN PLAYERS

Even though some African Americans played on college teams in the U.S. and Canada, many formed their own squads. Find out why and how some African-American teams lit up the court like no other.

CAN'T STOP US FROM HAVING A BALL

When basketball was invented, **racism** ruled much of North America. Many white people believed that the black race was inferior to the white race. Many places had regulations that didn't allow black people to go to the same schools, movies, or Ys as white people. By 1906, basketball was all the rage at African-American Ys. That year, the Smart Set Athletic Club of Brooklyn took to the court as the first organized African-American basketball team. African-American women's teams soon followed.

Though their schools and recreation centers were separate, African-American kids soon were playing basketball, too.

RISE OF THE RENS

In 1922, the all-black pro squad the Harlem Rens rose up. They went on tour, flattening almost all the competition. The Rens' games drew huge crowds and their games against the all-white Original Celtics drew thousands more. In 1925, the fierce rivals played six games. The Rens won three and the Celtics won three. That year, the American Basketball League invited the Celtics, the top white team, to join, but not the Rens, the top black team. To show support for the Rens, the Original Celtics turned down the invitation. But it wasn't until 1942 that pro basketball began to **integrate** black players.

During the 1932–33 regular season, the Rens won 88 games straight. That's twice as many as the Original Celtics' record of 44, and more than any other pro basketball team since.

PRINCES FROM HARLEM

In 1927, the Rens' success spurred another African-American team to form—the Harlem Globetrotters. The Globetrotters blew away almost all the competition. To keep people coming back to their games, they began clowning around and performing tricks. That's how they became known as the "Clown Princes of Basketball."

*Today's Globetrotters do not belong to a league. They play **exhibition games** as goodwill ambassadors for basketball.*

FIRST WORLD PRO BASKETBALL TOURNAMENT

In 1939, the Chicago Herald American newspaper held the first world tournament of pro basketball. The event was by invitation only and the competition was extreme.

AND THE WINNER IS...

Basketball fans couldn't wait for the action to begin. No matter whether they were black or white, the top teams in the U.S. were set to play in the tournament. The newspaper had invited the Celtics, the Rens, the Harlem Globetrotters, and the best teams of the pro leagues. In the semifinals, the Rens eliminated the Harlem Globetrotters. The Rens went on to beat the Oshkosh (Wisconsin) All Stars, 34 to 25, winning the tournament hands down.

The Chicago Coliseum (left) hosted some games for the World Professional Basketball Tournament. One of the top teams came from nearby. The Zollner Pistons from Fort Wayne, Indiana, won in 1944, 1945, and 1946. They are now the Detroit Pistons.

WORLD CHAMPIONS

In the eyes of basketball fans and pro players, winning the world tournament made the Rens the "World Champions of Basketball." The Harlem Globetrotters won that honor the next year, knocking out the Rens in the quarterfinals and edging out the Chicago Bruins in a nail-biting final that went into overtime. Pro teams went to battle at the tournament every year until 1949, when the National Basketball Association (NBA) arrived on the scene.

Bobby McDermott played five seasons for the Fort Wayne Zollner Pistons when they ruled pro basketball. The hall of famer was one of the first two players to average 20 points a game for a season. He was the MVP of the world tournament in 1944.

ON A ROLL

During that time, wheelchair basketball got rolling. On November 25, 1946, U.S. war veterans played the first game. Today, wheelchair basketball is a top sport of the Paralympic Summer Games.

Basketball is an exciting part of the U.S. Warrior Games for wounded and disabled military people. Special lightweight wheelchairs make for lots of action on the court.

THE NBA IS BORN

Pro basketball had been on shaky ground ever since it began. Several leagues had come and gone and basketball just didn't have the countless fans it does today. But all that was about to change.

NEW LEAGUE ON THE BLOCK

In 1946, the National Basketball League (NBL) was the major pro league in town. Nevertheless, it held many games in small gyms, church basements, and dance halls. A bunch of businessmen, who owned pro hockey arenas, were looking to make more money in the fall and winter. They thought adding pro basketball was just "the ticket." Not only had many star hoopsters just returned from World War II, but the businessmen thought basketball games in arenas could draw larger crowds than those that could squeeze into NBL games. With that, they formed the Basketball Association of America (BAA).

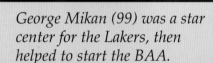

George Mikan (99) was a star center for the Lakers, then helped to start the BAA.

The Lakers were founded in 1947 in Minneapolis. They won six titles before moving to Los Angeles, where they have kept up their winning ways since 1960.

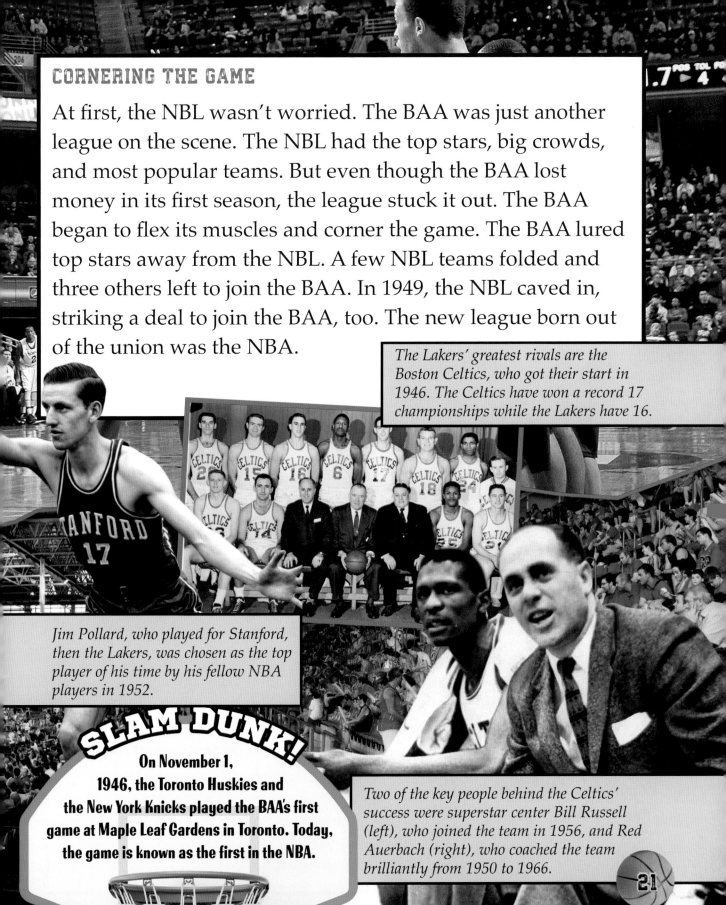

CORNERING THE GAME

At first, the NBL wasn't worried. The BAA was just another league on the scene. The NBL had the top stars, big crowds, and most popular teams. But even though the BAA lost money in its first season, the league stuck it out. The BAA began to flex its muscles and corner the game. The BAA lured top stars away from the NBL. A few NBL teams folded and three others left to join the BAA. In 1949, the NBL caved in, striking a deal to join the BAA, too. The new league born out of the union was the NBA.

The Lakers' greatest rivals are the Boston Celtics, who got their start in 1946. The Celtics have won a record 17 championships while the Lakers have 16.

Jim Pollard, who played for Stanford, then the Lakers, was chosen as the top player of his time by his fellow NBA players in 1952.

SLAM DUNK!

On November 1, 1946, the Toronto Huskies and the New York Knicks played the BAA's first game at Maple Leaf Gardens in Toronto. Today, the game is known as the first in the NBA.

Two of the key people behind the Celtics' success were superstar center Bill Russell (left), who joined the team in 1956, and Red Auerbach (right), who coached the team brilliantly from 1950 to 1966.

21

THE NBA GROWS

When the NBA was born, it was the only pro basketball game around. But eventually, some competition rolled into town.

B-BALL UPSTART

In 1967, the American Basketball Association (ABA) arrived. The ABA was the brainchild of **entrepreneur** Dennis Murphy. Murphy had a talent for promoting sports and a nose for opportunity. He believed that basketball had what it took to support a second pro league—enough interest, skilled players, and money to be made. Murphy drummed up the cash and the staff he needed. Then he launched the ABA with 11 teams.

Warren Jabali, who played guard, helped bring fans to the new ABA. He was Rookie of the Year in 1968–69 for the Oakland Oaks as they won the league title. By 1970, he had become an amazing three-point shooter as well.

NEW LEAGUE, NEW RULES

The ABA set itself apart from the start by using a red-white-and-blue ball. The ABA also brought in new rules that opened up the game and allowed flashier plays. For example, one new rule allowed three-point **field goals**. That way, players could score an extra point for netting the ball from any point beyond the arc around the basket. The ABA also allowed the **slam dunk**, in which players slam the ball down through the basket. Fans loved the freewheeling, loose, and **aggressive** playing style of the ABA and the NBA knew it. So when the NBA took over the ABA in 1976, it kept the new league's exciting plays.

Although the NBA first banned the slam, the league now has an annual Slam Dunk Contest.

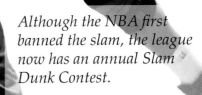

The NBA doubled in size as it competed with the ABA for new cities. Nine teams joined, including Portland (above) in 1970.

THE NBA TODAY

Even though all its teams are in North America, the NBA is the top basketball league on the planet. Here's how the top men's pro basketball league rules the court.

GOTTA BE TEAM PLAYERS

NBA teams roll into action with five players per side. To score points, all five players must work together and each has a main role to play. The point guard passes and handles the ball. The shooting guard shoots, passes, or **maneuvers** the ball to the basket and grabs **rebounds**. The small forward handles the ball and shoots to score from distances both near to and far from the basket. The power forward blocks shots, catches passes, and grabs rebounds. The center catches passes with his back to the basket, then **pivots**, or turns, to shoot as well as catch rebounds.

Houston's Dwight Howard is 6 feet 11 inches (2.1 m)—that's average for NBA centers. Teams count on their center's height.

TALE OF TWO 'HOODS

The NBA has 30 teams. Depending on its 'hood, each team belongs to the Eastern Conference or the Western Conference. Each conference has 15 teams, which are divided into three groups of five teams each. These groups are called **divisions**. The Eastern Conference holds the Atlantic, Central, and Southeast divisions. The Western Conference includes the Pacific, Northwest, and Southwest divisions.

GOING FOR THE TROPHY

The road to an NBA title is a long one. Players tune up with exhibition games in October. The regular season starts at the end of the month and runs through mid-April. Every team plays 41 games at home and 41 on the road, including at least two games against every other team in the league.

The excitement builds in late April, when the playoffs begin. Eight teams in each conference make the playoffs. By June, only two are left. The two conference champions play in the NBA Finals for the Larry O'Brien Trophy and bragging rights as the best basketball team in the world.

Larry O'Brien was the NBA commissioner, or director, from 1975 to 1984. The championship trophy was named after him in 1984.

WOMEN'S BASKETBALL

According to inventor James Naismith, basketball wasn't even a month old before women took it up. Here's how the women's game caught fire and spread.

GAME ONE

One day in 1892, a few women, who were regulars at the Y and taught at a school nearby, heard shouts coming from the gym. They popped their heads in to see what was going on and caught their first glimpse of basketball. The women were intrigued on the spot. They asked Naismith to teach them how to play and he agreed. A few months later, the first game between two women's teams took place.

In early basketball, women wore divided skirts called bloomers to play in.

Berenson's work earned her a spot in the Hall of Fame.

WOMEN OWN THE GAME

In 1893, Senda Berenson, the director of physical education at Smith College, discovered basketball and taught it to women at the college in Massachusetts. She also helped women make the game their own by **adapting** some of the rules. For example, Berenson divided the court into three sections and had each person play only in their assigned section. She also outlawed seizing the ball, holding the ball for more than three seconds, and dribbling it more than three times. The women's game spread like wildfire. By 1895, women's basketball was being played across the continent.

A RULE BOOK OF THEIR OWN

As women's basketball grew popular, official rules were needed. A Women's Basketball Rules Committee was created in 1899 to write a rule book based on Berenson's ideas. Official rule books were published from 1901 until 1917 by Spalding, a sporting goods company. By the 1960s, the rules for the women's game had become very similar to those of men's basketball.

The 1915 Spalding's Women's Basket Ball Guide.

MODERN WOMEN'S BASKETBALL

What sets basketball apart from all other major league sports such as football, hockey, and even baseball? It's the only sport with organized teams for girls all the way from high school to college to the pro level—the Women's National Basketball Association (WNBA).

GIRL, CAN YOU EVER PLAY!

In basketball, girls and women have the opportunity to take their game to the highest level. Women's basketball has been an official Olympic sport since 1976. The college game took a little longer. In 1972, the U.S. adopted a law to make sure girls had equal access to sports. More girls began playing college ball, and the NCAA started sponsoring women's basketball in 1982. Today, women's college basketball is just as popular with fans as the men's college game.

The women's NCAA tournament is held at the same time as the men's. In 2004 and 2014, the University of Connecticut took home both championships!

THE WNBA

Fans **clamored** for more action, so the WNBA was born. In 1996, the WNBA provided women with a pro league of their own. The U.S. women's national team won games around the world, then won Olympic gold in Atlanta. Today, the WNBA has 12 teams, many star players, and tons of fans.

Sue Bird is a basketball star! She is one of nine women to win an Olympic gold medal, an NCAA championship, and a WNBA championship. In 2011, fans voted Bird as one of the WNBA's Top 15 Players of All Time.

SLAM DUNK!

In 1976, women's basketball became an Olympic sport. The Soviet Union won the gold, the U.S. the silver, and Bulgaria the bronze.

WOMEN HAVE A BALL

The WNBA's ball has orange and white stripes and is slightly smaller than the ball used by the NBA. The women's three-point line is also closer to the basket than the men's line. In the WNBA, the 3-point line is 19 feet 9 inches (6 meters) from the basket. The distance in the NBA is 23 ft 9 in (7.25 m). The WNBA games are shorter, too. The NBA games are 48 minutes long, the WNBA games last only 40 minutes. But apart from these and a few other differences, modern women's basketball is played with almost the same rules as men's basketball.

BASKETBALL AROUND THE WORLD

Name any country and you can bet basketball is played there. Basketball is a global game. Just look at the number of NBA players who come from different countries around the world!

GET IN THE GAME

Whether you want to be a future b-ball superstar or just have fun, there are lots of opportunities to play basketball. All you need is a ball, a hoop, and some sneakers. You can shoot hoops indoors or outdoors, on your own, with a friend, or with a couple of friends. You can also join an organized team at the Y, or a local league.

Basketball caught on quickly in Europe, where clubs today compete on three levels called Euroleague, Eurocup, and Eurochallenge.

LEARNING MORE

Check out these books and websites to find out more about the basketball.

BOOKS

The Man Who Invented the Game of Basketball: The Genius of James Naismith by Edwin Brit Wyckoff, Enslow Elementary, 2013

Sports Illustrated Kids Slam Dunk!: Top 10 Lists of Everything in Basketball by The Editors of Sports Illustrated Kids, Sports Illustrated, 2014

The Best of Everything Basketball Book (The All-Time Best of Sports) by Nate LeBoutillier, Capstone Press, 2014

WEBSITES

NBA History

www.nba.com/history

Visit this site to see an interactive timeline, and read profiles, and watch videos of NBA legends.

Basketball Hall of Fame

www.hoophall.com

The best of the best will be remembered forever in the Naismith Memorial Basketball Hall of Fame. Learn more about your favorite hall of famers here.

GLOSSARY

Note: Some boldfaced words are defined where they appear in the book.

adapting Changing something to fit a new use or situation

aggressive Ready to attack, forceful

clamored Made a loud and continuous noise

entrepreneur A person who organizes and manages a business

exclusive Restricted or limited

exhibition game A game that does not count toward a team's regular season record

field goal A basket scored on any shot other than a free throw

folded (sports) Stopped operating due to financial trouble or lack of support

free throws A shot that has been awarded for a penalty and is taken from the freethrow line;. worth one point.

hazards Things that are potentially dangerous

integrate To unite into a whole, to end racial separation

makeshift Temporary and quickly put together

maneuver To make a planned move, often one that is skillful or clever

racism A belief that one race is superior, or hatred or discrimination based on race

rebound To gain possession of the basketball after a missed shot

roman balcony A platform inside a building that extends out over part of the main floor

slam dunk A shot made by a player who jumps in the air and puts the ball directly in the basket; "Slam dunk" now is used to describe a sure thing

unruly Disruptive and unorganized

YMCA Young Men's Christian Association, an organization that promotes health and welfare. Its programs now serve people of all faiths and ages.

INDEX